CHARCOAL COMPANION

SALT PLATE
RECIPE BOOK

COOKING AND SERVING WITH A NATURAL SALT PLATE

©2014 The Companion Group

Berkeley, California

800-521-0505

www.companion-group.com

INTRODUCTION

APPETIZERS

MAINS

DESSERTS

INTRODUCTION

Salt's historical significance is fascinating. This mineral compound's complex history stretches over millennia with evidence of its use as currency amongst Phoenicians in prehistoric times. References to salt are also abundant in a wide variety of religious texts. Salt was used globally to preserve and cure foods before the invention of refrigeration. It has been the cause of numerous wars, served as a symbol of political power for many empires and regimes, and has played an important role in determining the development of a hundreds of cities and civilizations around the world.

Himalayan salt, a result of millions of years in the making, is harvested in the form of boulders from ancient salt mines in the far reaches of the Himalayas. The salt boulders are then crafted into individual blocks to be used in a myriad of manners, including an emerging tool of modern cookery: the salt plate.

This gorgeous pink salt is so much more than ordinary table salt. In fact, it's composed of up to 82 trace minerals, all of which function together to aid in the body's proper metabolic performance. This network of minerals also helps strengthen bones, harmonizes with water in the body to help maintain blood pressure, and aids the body in absorbing more nutrients during digestion.

Cooking on a Himalayan salt plate adds enormous depth of flavor to foods without over-salting. And thanks to naturally low moisture content, Himalayan salt plates can be heated or chilled to extreme temperatures. The salt plate works beautifully on the grill, on the stove top, in the oven and even as a serving platter for cold food presentations.

The possibilities for cooking with Himalayan salt are endless. The recipes in this book showcase the use of a salt plate in different capacities, from hot to cold dishes, appetizer to dessert. Most recipes are written for two servings and can be easily scaled to feed a larger group. Use the recipes not only as a guide to cook each dish, but also as an inspiration to further experiment.

THE SALT PLATE IN USE

It may be a concern that cooking on a salt plate will make foods too salty. Of course, there is a bit of a learning curve when it comes to cooking on a salt plate, but keeping a few considerations in mind will drastically cut down on the chance of serving overly salty foods.

How long will food need to cook?

The longer the food is in contact with the salt plate, the more salt will be imparted onto the food. Keep these tips in mind:

- Adequately preheat the salt plate before use to avoid longer cooking times
- Avoid bone-in cuts, excluding fish
- Use smaller, more uniform cuts for ingredients

How much moisture exists naturally in the food?

High moisture ingredients will pull more salt from the plate. If possible, pat ingredients with a paper towel beforehand to absorb some moisture. Also, keep in mind that fat resists salt. If foods come off the plate too salty, add a layer of neutral cooking oil directly to the salt plate.

How hot (or cold) is the salt plate?

Cooking at the proper temperature is the most important guideline to follow when working with a salt plate. It is imperative to take the time to properly and adequately preheat the salt plate, whether on the grill, on the stove top or in the oven. Failure to do so may result in salty food and could effect the integrity of the salt plate.

Some of these factors are obvious, while others are not. Regardless, it is a good idea to consider these factors before beginning to cook with the salt plate. Salting your food while cooking is so routine, that it may take several attempts with the salt plate to remember to "hold the salt!"

COLD FOOD PRESENTATIONS

Salt plates make great serving trays – not only are they beautiful, but they can also season foods in an unexpectedly pleasant way! Keep a salt plate in the fridge for serving cheese plates, salads, and sushi. Keep another one in the freezer to serve gelato, sorbet, or other frozen treats.

HEATING THE SALT PLATE

The thermal qualities of a Himalayan salt plate make for an ideal cooking surface to sear, bake, and roast a wide variety of proteins, vegetables, and fruits. Furthermore, the salt plate can be heated and used as a press to speed up the process of roasting larger cuts of meat.

Salt plates can be used on the grill, on the stove top, or in the oven. Regardless of the cooking appliance, the salt plate is susceptible to thermal shock (breaking due to dramatic changes in temperature), and must be brought to its ideal temperature in stages. All preheating instructions follow the same three-phase preheat of starting with low heat for 15 minutes, then turning it up to medium heat for 15 minutes, and finally finishing with high heat for another 15 minutes.

Follow these guidelines to safely preheat a salt plate:

Be sure to handle the heated salt plate carefully, as it will be extremely hot. You may use a salt plate holder with handles, specifically designed for this purpose, as well as heavy-duty oven mitts.

It's a good idea to check the surface temperature of the salt plate with an infrared thermometer before placing food onto the surface for cooking. The salt plate will maintain its temperature for quite some time, but please keep in mind that if you are cooking multiple batches, foods will acquire saltier flavor as the plate cools. The hotter your salt plate is, the less salt your food will pick up.

Please note that as the salt plate warms, it will discolor slightly, changing from translucent pink to opaque, sometimes an ash gray. This is completely normal and does not affect the performance of the salt plate.

Electric or Gas Range: When using a salt plate on an electric range, you'll need something heat safe to elevate the salt so it sits just above the burner. We recommend using a cake or pastry ring. Place the ring over the burner, set your salt plate on top and begin preheating. If you're using a gas range, simply place the salt plate on your burner with the grate in place, and begin preheating.

While setting up for cooking with a salt plate can be different with gas and electric ranges, the act of preheating is the same. Once you've set up your plate, simply follow the directions below to preheat:

Start with the plate on low for 15 minutes, then set the burner to medium for 15 minutes, then turn the burner up to high (if high heat is needed) and finish preheating another 15 minutes.

Outdoor Grill:
Gas: Place your salt plate parallel over a burner bar on the grill grate. Preheat by starting the plate on low for 15 minutes, then turn up the burner to medium for 15 minutes, then finish with the burner on high (if high heat is needed) for another 15 minutes. Feel free to close the grill hood after you've ensured that the burner has been lit for the first phase of preheating.

Charcoal: Set up your grill with three separate heat zones. On the far left side of your grill there should be open space, with no charcoal. In the middle of your grill place a single layer of lit charcoal, and on the far right side of your grill place a double layer of charcoal. Once the charcoal is lit and the grill is configured, start with your salt plate on the left for 15 minutes, move it to the middle for 15 minutes, and finish on the far right side for another 15 minutes.

Oven: Place your salt plate into the oven. Preheat at 250° F for 15 minutes, then increase the temperature to 325° F for 15 minutes, and again to 400° F for the final 15 minutes. Use of the salt plate under a broiler is not recommended.

CARE AND MAINTENANCE

Proper care will greatly extend the life of a salt plate. Himalayan salt is naturally antimicrobial and requires no cleaning chemicals. After use, simply wash the salt plate under a thin stream of warm water and scrub lightly with a soft brush or sponge. Take care to work efficiently as the longer the plate is in contact with water or a brush, the more salt is washed away. By all means, do not submerge the plate in water! Dry with a paper towel to remove any excess pockets of water in the plate. Air-dry the plate for at least 24 hours before the next use.

Proper storage of the salt plate is also important in its longevity. Store the salt plate in a dry environment after cleaning and drying. Take caution with metal surfaces, as the salt will tend to rust things made from steel. If possible, purchase a carrying case for the salt plate to avoid scratching or rusting any surfaces that may come into contact with it. A carrying case also aids in transportation while also protecting it from absorbing excess moisture.

With proper care, your salt plate will last for many, many uses. However, over time and with use, it will slowly break apart and dissolve. Using a grid or holder designed specifically for salt plates will not only protect the plate during use but also serve as a frame to hold together larger pieces of salt once it starts to break apart.

Once the plate becomes too small for cooking, the remaining salt can be ground or grated for sprinkling on foods!

APPETIZERS

GRILL BAKED BRIE WITH ALMONDS

This dish is an absolutely gooey cheesy dream come true. Rich and creamy brie warmed just to the point of beginning to melt, marries with the subtle saltiness of the plate for a delectable appetizer to feed a crowd. Change things up a bit and serve with sliced apples or figs, and by all means, don't forget the wine!

Ingredients:

1 wheel	Brie or Camembert cheese
1	baguette or other crusty bread
2 Tbsp.	extra-virgin olive oil
¼ c.	smokehouse almonds, coarsely chopped
¼ c.	dried or fresh figs, apple or pear slices

Method:

Cut the baguette diagonally into ¼ inch thick slices and brush with olive oil. Toast the baguette slices on a grill over medium-low heat 2-3 minutes per side or until golden brown.

Preheat salt plate on grill on low for 30 minutes. Once pre-heated to 200º F, place the wheel of brie centered onto the salt plate, and close the lid. Cook for 20-30 minutes or until cheese wheel just breaks open and is heated throughout. Carefully remove hot salt plate from the grill and place on a heat-safe serving surface. Sprinkle with crushed smokehouse almonds, figs and remaining olive oil. Serve with toasted baguette slices.

Tip: Serve the appetizer immediately after the cheese breaks open from the heat of the grill. Cheese that sits too long on the plate will be overly salty. If using something other than brie or camembert, consider the saltiness of the cheese before purchasing it. Most gourmet markets have someone tending the cheese counter that may have valuable advice about the saltiness of a particular cheese.

TEQUILA LIME SHRIMP

This refreshingly light dish is perfect for a warm summer evening. In this recipe, the salt plate acts as a plancha, effectively searing the shrimp's exterior with a delicious, crispy crust while keeping the interior moist and perfectly seasoned. Pair with a green salad and don't forget to bring the margaritas!

Shrimp Ingredients:

1 lb.	large shrimp, peeled, deveined
6	wooden skewers (10 inch)
2 Tbsp.	lime juice, fresh squeezed
2 Tbsp.	tequila
¼ c.	olive oil
1 large	garlic clove, minced
1 pinch	ground cumin
1 pinch	ground coriander
1 pinch	dried oregano
	ground black pepper to taste
1 large	lime, quartered

Fresh Cilantro Pico Ingredients:

1 med.	tomato, small dice
¼ med	red onion, finely chopped
2 Tbsp.	cilantro, finely chopped
1 pinch	salt and pepper

Method:

Combine marinade ingredients in a medium sized bowl and mix to incorporate. Reserve 1 tablespoon of marinade. Finely chop tomato, red onion and cilantro. Combine finely chopped vegetables with reserved marinade.

Combine remaining marinade and shrimp in a Ziploc bag or Tupperware container and marinade 2-4 hours. Preheat salt plate on grill as recommended on page 6. Drain shrimp from excess marinade and place on skewers. When salt plate is fully preheated, place skewered shrimp on plate and cook 1-2 minutes per side. When shrimp have finished cooking, remove from plate and serve with fresh cilantro pico.

GRILLED CAPRESE ON THE VINE

Undoubtedly, one of summer's greatest treats is a fresh tomato from
the garden. Use your salt plate to bring out the natural sweetness of the
tomato by searing the bottoms and cooking them just enough to make this
dish melt-in-your mouth delicious. Pair with your favorite crusty bread for
an elegantly easy appetizer.

Ingredients:

3 small	tomatoes, attached by the stems
1-1½ ball	fresh mozzarella or burrata (approximately 8 oz.)
½ c.	fresh basil leaves
	extra-virgin olive oil

Method:

Preheat salt plate on grill as recommended on page 6. When salt plate is preheated,
carefully slice bottoms of tomatoes so that they will sit flat and sear on the salt plate.
Place the bunch of 3 tomatoes, still on vine on the hot salt plate to sear the bottom of the
tomatoes. Once bottoms of tomatoes have been cooked (about 12-15 minutes), remove
tomatoes from salt plate and serve plated with sliced mozzarella and freshly basil leaves.

*Tip: Don't let the tomatoes sit too long on the plate after cooking, or they may end up too
salty.*

LATKES WITH LAMB SAUSAGE AND BLACK TRUFFLE OIL

Traditionally, latkes are fried to achieve a crispy exterior. Here, we eliminate the oil and sear bake the potato cakes on a piping hot salt plate. Served alongside grilled lamb sausages with a drizzle of black truffle oil, this dish is perfect to share as an appetizer or pair with a salad for a light meal. Russet or Yukon Gold potatoes work best in this recipe.

Ingredients:

2 c.	potatoes, peeled and shredded
¼ c.	onion, grated
2 Tbsp.	chives, thinly sliced crosswise
2 small	eggs, beaten
1 Tbsp.	all-purpose flour
2 links	lamb sausage, sliced crosswise at an angle
1 tsp.	black truffle oil
2 Tbsp.	sour cream

Method:

Preheat salt plate on grill as recommended on page 6. Meanwhile, shred potatoes using the large holes of a cheese grater. Place shredded potatoes in bowl filled with ice water for 30 minutes.

Remove potatoes from ice water and squeeze by hand to remove excess liquid and set aside. After removing potatoes, slowly drain bowl of ice water being careful not to disturb the settled potato starch at the bottom of the bowl. Mix potatoes with grated onion, eggs, truffle oil, flour and reserved potato starch. When salt plate has fully preheated, scoop 3 ounces potato batter onto hot salt plate and cook 3-4 minutes until browned and the edges are crisp. Flip and cook another 3-4 minutes or until golden and crispy.

Grill sliced lamb sausage on a grilling grid over direct heat while the latkes are cooking on the salt plate, 2-4 minutes per side or until cooked through. Serve sausages over latkes with sour cream and chives. Garnish with additional truffle oil, if desired.

Yield: 6 latkes

SEARED SCALLOPS WITH BLOOD ORANGE AND AVOCADO SALAD

Searing a scallop can be an intimidating task, especially if you've tried once before and failed. The trick is to make sure the scallop is dry and that the pan is hot. In this recipe, we've replaced the pan with a blazing hot salt plate, which as in other recipes, works as a plancha to sear in flavor and moisture. Serve your perfectly seared scallops atop a light, citrusy avocado salad. Don't worry if you can't find blood oranges; grapefruit is a suitable and just as delicious substitution.

Ingredients:

6-8 large	sea scallops (under 15 per pound), patted dry
2 med.	handfuls mixed greens, washed and dry
1 large	avocado
1 med.	blood orange
1 Tbsp.	extra-virgin olive oil
	black pepper

Method:

Preheat salt plate on grill as recommended on page 6.

Peel and slice avocado in half. Slice half avocado into strips, placing strips on serving plates. Zest and peel blood orange, separating orange slices from pith. Place half of the blood orange pieces on plate alternating between slices of avocado. Squeeze juice from remaining blood orange pieces and mix with 1 Tbsp. of extra-virgin olive oil. Dress mixed greens with the blood orange vinaigrette and place on serving plates with avocado and orange slices.

When plate is fully preheated, sprinkle scallops with pepper and place flat side down on the plate. Scallops should take 1-2 minutes to brown nicely on each side. Serve scallops medium rare or desired temperature over avocado and oranges.

BEEF TARTARE

Steak tartare, when prepared well, is perfectly seasoned and tender beef at its best. To succeed with this recipe, use only the highest quality beef tenderloin you can find, preferably from a reputable local butcher. Make sure your knife is sharp and by all means, keep the ingredients chilled until just before use. A bit of attention to detail may result in a new favorite beef dish!

Ingredients:

10 oz.	beef tenderloin
½	baguette, sweet or sourdough
2 Tbsp.	lemon oil
2	quail eggs
1 head	frisée lettuce
1 ½ tsp.	red wine vinegar
1 Tbsp.	extra-virgin olive oil
2 Tbsp.	horseradish mustard
6	cornichons
1	ring mold, for shaping beef

Method:

Chill a salt plate in the freezer for at least 30 minutes, but preferably 2-3 hours prior to serving. Slice the baguette on the bias into at least eight pieces. Brush baguette slices with 1 Tbsp. lemon oil and toast under the broiler until evenly browned. Set aside.

Trim any excess sinew or large pieces of fat from the chilled beef tenderloin. Cut beef into tiny cube shaped pieces and mix with 1 Tbsp. lemon oil.

To assemble for serving, place seasoned beef into ring mold on the chilled salt plate, gently packing it in. Slide the mold upwards to remove it from the plate. With a paring knife, remove top portion of quail egg shell and place on top of beef. Trim green ends from frisee and toss with olive oil and red wine vinegar. Arrange with toasted baguette, salad, horseradish mustard and cornichons. To begin, simply pour the quail eggs onto the beef and mix on the salt plate.

MAINS

HANGAR STEAK WITH EXOTIC MUSHROOMS AND GREEN BEANS

Once a treasured secret among butchers, the hangar (skirt) steak is now world-renowned for being extremely tender and flavorful. Just a few minutes per side on the salt plate is all it takes to bring this magical cut of beef to life. Served with an earthy blend of grilled exotic mushrooms and crisp, charred long beans you will find this recipe to be a satisfying, protein-rich feast.

Ingredients:

1	hangar steak, trimmed and cut into four pieces
¾ lb.	green and/or yellow long beans, stems removed
½ lb.	baby sunburst squash
½ stick	salted butter
2 Tbsp.	garlic, minced
8 oz.	chef's mix mushrooms (enoki, piopini, chantrelle or oyster), coarsely chopped
1 Tbsp.	extra-virgin olive oil
	black pepper to taste
	kosher salt to taste

Method:

Preheat salt plate on grill as recommended on page 6.

Remove stems from green beans and slice baby squash in half. Blanch green beans in boiling water 1-2 minutes until they have been half-cooked. After removing beans from boiling water, place them in a bowl with ice water to stop the cooking process. Melt butter in a pot with garlic, pepper, and a pinch of salt. Cook over low flame until garlic becomes fragrant, 2-3 minutes. Combine beans and squash in a medium sized bowl and coat with the garlic/butter mixture. Set aside. Toss mushrooms with olive oil and salt and place them in a hot grill wok or grill basket. Cook mushrooms until they begin to brown and become soft. Remove mushrooms and place them in a foil pouch so they can be reheated as soon as the steaks are nearly done.

Add pepper to hangar steaks and coat lightly with extra-virgin olive oil. When salt plate is fully preheated, place hangar steaks on plate. Cook approximately 3-4 minutes per side for medium rare; longer for more well done steaks. While steaks are cooking, add squash/beans to hot grill work and cook 8-10 minutes over high flame. If desired, coat beans/squash with additional garlic butter when finished. Dress steaks with cooked mushrooms for serving.

Tip: If the local market doesn't carry a pre-packaged mushroom mix, simply pick three different varieties of mushrooms and purchase just under ¼ lb. each.

HOISIN PORK BELLY WITH BABY BOK CHOY

Pork belly, a traditional favorite of Chinese and Korean cuisine, is gaining popularity in the USA. Typically prepared by braising (low and slow in a flavorful liquid) this recipe uses the salt plate as a meat press to speed up the cooking process. The blazing hot salt plate pressed onto the meat works to render fat from the pork belly while perfectly seasoning the meat and crisping the exterior.

Pork Ingredients:

1¼ lbs.	pork belly, with skin
½ Tbsp.	Japanese cooking wine (Mirin)
½ tsp.	Five-spice powder
½ tsp.	ground black pepper
1 Tbsp.	hoisin sauce

Bok Choy Ingredients:

4 bunches	baby bok choy, cut in half
1 Tbsp.	olive oil
1 ½ tsp.	sesame oil
½ tsp.	toasted sesame oil
½ tsp.	dried red chili flakes
3	garlic cloves, sliced
1 ½ tsp.	fresh ginger, grated
	kosher salt to taste
	pepper to taste

Method:

Brush pork with cooking wine and season with five-spice powder and black pepper. Cover and let rest in refrigerator for 12 hours.

Preheat salt plate on grill as recommended on page 6. Remove meat from refrigerator. Using three sharp metal skewers pierce the skin of the pork belly across entire surface. Holes should penetrate skin but not go into the fat of the pork.

Once salt plate is preheated, brush the pork again with cooking wine and place under salt plate or a cookie sheet. Roast over indirect heat on the grill, hood closed, at 400° F for 45-50 minutes.

Meanwhile, blanch the bok choy halves in boiling water until almost fully cooked, approximately 2-3 minutes. Drain bok choy and move immediately to an ice water bath. Once cooled, remove from ice water and dry with a paper towel. Set aside.

Once the pork reaches an internal temperature of 145° F remove it from the grill. Remove the salt plate and transfer the pork belly to the oven and broil for 5-10 minutes or until the skin is crisp and bubbly. After the skin is crisp, sauté chili flake, garlic, and ginger in a skillet over medium high heat for 30 seconds then add blanched bok choy and continue to cook until hot throughout, 2-3 minutes. To serve, brush pork belly with hoisin sauce, slice and arrange over vegetables.

SALT PLATE PIZZA MARGHERITA

The thermal quality of a salt plate makes for an ideal surface to bake fresh dough, most especially pizza dough. Take the time to properly preheat the salt plates and use an infrared thermometer to verify the surface temperature has reached 500° F. Doing so will ensure a crisp and delicious crust each and every time.

Ingredients:

1 ball	pizza dough (8-10 oz.)
4 oz.	pizza sauce
1 ball	fresh mozzarella cheese (approximately 8 oz.), torn into pieces
1 handfull	fresh basil leaves
	extra-virgin olive oil

Method:

Place two 8 x 12 inch salt plates, side by side on the grill and preheat on grill as recommended on page 6. When the surface temperature of the salt plates reach 500° F, it is time to bake.

Stretch the pizza dough to approximately ¼ inch thickness. Place on a floured pizza peel and garnish with sauce and mozzarella. Verify the grill temperature is 400° F or above and transfer the pizza to the preheated salt plates. Bake approximately 12-18 minutes or until the crisp is crust and the toppings are golden bubbly. Garnish with fresh basil and a drizzle of extra-virgin olive oil just before serving.

Tip: Using truffle infused mozzarella adds an amazing twist to this classic pizza.

SEARED AHI TUNA
WITH WASABI POTATO SALAD

A salt plate is ideal for flash-cooking delicate foods, most especially fish. Tuna, at its best served raw or very rare, in this recipe is seared on a salt plate to maintain the integrity of the fish while adding an additional layer of subtle flavor. Served warm aside a cool wasabi infused potato salad, this recipe is a great example of true California cuisine.

Ingredients:

12 oz.	sushi grade ahi tuna, divided into two equal portions
1 Tbsp. + 1 tsp.	prepared wasabi
1 ¼ lbs.	red potatoes, scrubbed and eyes removed
½ c.	aioli or mayonnaise
2 Tbsp.	buttermilk
1 tsp.	fresh dill, finely chopped
¼ c.	Chinese celery, finely diced
¼ c.	red onion, finely diced
	kosher salt to taste
	fresh ground pepper to taste
	wasabi tobiko (optional, for garnish)

Method:

Put the potatoes in a large pot, cover with cold water and bring to a boil over medium-high heat. Cook until a knife inserted into the center of the potatoes meets little resistance, but they still hold their shape. Do not overcook. Carefully drain the potatoes, let cool to room temperature, and refrigerate for at least 2 hours or overnight.

Halve the potatoes lengthwise and then slice into pieces (thickness is up to you). Combine together the potatoes, celery, onion, pepper (to taste) and dill in a large mixing bowl. In a separate bowl, combine mayo, buttermilk, half the wasabi, and salt– then whisk until incorporated. Taste mixture for heat and add more wasabi if desired. Add this mixture to bowl containing potatoes and celery, and mix until salad is formed. Refrigerate until ready to serve.

Preheat salt plate on grill as recommended on page 6. Salt plate should be 600-650° F before cooking. When plate is fully preheated, sprinkle tuna with pepper and place flat side down on the plate. Tuna should take 2-3 minutes to brown nicely on each side. Serve tuna sliced over potato salad with tobiko garnish.

Tip: Chinese celery has a stronger flavor than normal celery. Look for it in an Asian market, otherwise substitute with normal celery.

BEEF FAJITAS WITH CITRUS CHIMICHURRI

Serving the steak with a bright citrus chimichurri sauce adds an enormous amount of flavor and creates a delicious contrast of sweet and savory. Paired with lightly charred onions, peppers and tortillas, these beef fajitas become the centerpiece of an easy weeknight fiesta!

Fajitas Ingredients:

1-1.5 lb.	flank or skirt steak, sliced ¼ inch thick pieces
3 small	bell peppers (red, yellow, green) sliced julienne style
1 small	red onion, cut into quarters sliced julienne style
6	corn or flour tortillas
3 oz.	fajita spice mix

Chimichurri Ingredients:

¼ c.	cilantro
¼ c.	parsley, Italian flat leaf
1 Tbsp.	lemon juice
1 ½ tsp.	red wine vinegar
½ c.	olive oil
½ tsp.	dried red chili flakes
½ tsp.	kosher salt
1 large	orange, zest removed and juiced
1	garlic clove, minced

Method:

Finely mince cilantro, parsley, and garlic and combine in a large bowl. Zest orange and extract juice. Mince 2 tsp. orange zest and add to bowl with ¼ cup of orange juice. Add remaining chimichurri ingredients into bowl and mix until combined.

Preheat salt plate on grill as recommended on page 6.

Meanwhile, grill sliced onion and bell peppers in a grill wok or basket directly over high heat. Set aside. Grill tortillas 10-15 seconds on each side until slightly charred and heated through, then wrap in foil to keep warm.

Season the meat with fajita spice mix and brush with olive oil. Place steak on hot salt plate and cook 1-2 minutes per side. Serve fajitas with freshly made chimichurri, grilled peppers and warm tortillas.

Tip: The steak can be cooked entirely on the grill, or at table side (on a heat-safe surface), for a more interactive meal. The plate will remain hot enough to cook several servings, but may have to be reheated if it cools down too much.

BRICK ROASTED CHICKEN
WITH MARBLED POTATOES

"Pollo Al Mattone" is the Italian tradition of cooking chicken under a brick. While this may seem a strange concept, pressing the bird under a heavy object effectively crisps the skin and sears in moisture resulting in the most succulent chicken imaginable. In this recipe, a salt plate serves as a brick while adding an additional seasoning boost and maintaining maximum moisture. And if halving a chicken seems intimidating, ask the butcher to do it for you.

Chicken Ingredients:

1	half chicken
4	garlic cloves, coarsely chopped
1 Tbsp.	lemon thyme, chopped
1 large	lemon, juiced
½ tsp.	dried red chili flakes
1 Tbsp.	Meyer lemon oil
	black pepper to taste

Potatoes Ingredients:

1 ½ lbs.	marbled potatoes, rinsed
¼ lb.	baby onions
3 Tbsp.	roasted garlic oil

Method:

Combine lemon thyme, lemon juice, red chili flakes, lemon oil and ground black pepper in a small bowl. Place the half chicken into a zip closure plastic bag and add marinade. Lay the bag with chicken and marinade flat on a plate and place in the refrigerator for 2-4 hours, turning the bag once during the marinating process.

Preheat salt plate on grill as recommended on page 6. While the salt plate is preheating, slice potatoes in half and peel onions. Toss potatoes in roasted garlic oil with salt, pepper and onions. Set aside.

When the salt plate is fully preheated, turn off half of the burners and place the chicken skin side down on a well-oiled grill grate over indirect heat. Place roasting dish with potatoes and onions next to chicken over low flame until potatoes are fork tender. Rotate chicken 45° after 2 minutes to complete grill marks. Place salt plate on top of chicken and cook 10-15 minutes per side or until an internal temperature of 165° F is reached. Remove chicken from the grill and allow it to rest while the potatoes finish cooking. Serve the chicken on a platter surrounded by roasted potatoes, onions and any accumulated juices from the cutting board.

LAMB CHOPS WITH TABBOULEH

The chef's motto "salt + fat = flavor" never rang truer than when fire roasting a rack of lamb. Lamb, naturally rich in fat, cooks perfectly on a salt plate, searing in loads of flavor and forming an irresistible crust. The North African inspired spice rub in this recipe, paired with a crisp, fresh tabbouleh salad makes for an elegant meal perfect for entertaining.

Lamb Chops Ingredients:

1 small	rack of lamb, cut into two pieces

Harissa Dry Spice Mix Ingredients:

4 tsp.	cumin seed		3 tsp.	smoked paprika
4 tsp.	coriander seed		½ tsp.	sea salt
1 tsp.	caraway seeds		1½ tsp.	garlic powder
4 Tbsp.	dried Arbol chili pepper, roughly chopped			

Method:

Begin by preparing Tabbouleh; recipe is on the following page.

To prepare Harissa Dry Spice Mix, place cumin, coriander, caraway seeds, and chili into a sauté pan and toast over medium heat until fragrant. Take care not to burn the seeds. Remove from heat and cool completely. Place all the seeds in a mortar and pestle or dedicated coffee grinder, and grind until coarse. Mix in remaining ingredients. Spice mix is best made a few days ahead of time.

Rub lamb racks with harissa spice mix and brush with olive oil. Set aside.

Preheat salt plate on grill as recommended on page 6. Once pre-heated, place the lamb onto the salt plate and sear on all sides, approximately 3-4 minutes per side. Remove from salt plate and allow to rest, for 5 minutes. Slice lamb rack between the bones and serve over tabbouleh.

Tip: Harissa can also be purchased pre-made to save time. If using Harissa paste be sure to brush the paste onto the meat in the final few minutes of cooking.

LAMB CHOPS WITH TABBOULEH (CONTINUED)

Tabbouleh Salad Ingredients:

¼ c.	bulgar
¼ c. + 1 Tbsp.	boiling water
1 Tbsp. + 1 tsp.	olive oil
1 Tbsp. + 1 tsp.	lemon juice
3 Tbsp.	shallots, minced
½ c.	fresh parsley, finely chopped
2 Tbsp.	fresh mint, finely chopped
¾ c.	cherry tomatoes, halved
½ c.	English cucumber, seeded and chopped
¼ tsp.	kosher salt
	ground black pepper to taste

Method:

Boil water, then pour over dry bulgar and steep 1 to 1 ½ hours until soft. Squeeze out excess water from bulgar using hands or paper towel. Once bulgar has cooled, add shallots, parsley, mint, tomatoes, and cucumber; mix thoroughly. Add olive oil, lemon juice, salt and freshly ground pepper to taste. Stir until well combined and refrigerate covered until ready to serve.

SALT PLATE PORK TENDERLOIN WITH FENNEL APPLE SLAW

The key to successfully cooking pork tenderloin is not to overcook it. Use your salt plate to sear the exterior and lightly season the meat while it cooks to perfection in only a few minutes per side. Served with a tart and crispy slaw, this healthy entrée is perfect for any night of the week.

Ingredients:

1	pork tenderloin cut into two 8-10 oz. pieces
1 small	green apple, sliced (Granny Smith, Gala or other tart, crisp variety)
1 bulb	fennel
2 c.	wild arugula
2 Tbsp.	extra-virgin olive oil
1½ tsp.	apple cider vinegar
	salt
	pepper

Method:

Preheat salt plate on grill as recommended on page 6. Season the tenderloin with pepper and brush lightly with olive oil. Once preheated, place the tenderloin on the plate and sear until it browns on one side. After searing one side flip the loin and reduce heat from high to medium flame. Cook approximately 6-8 minutes per side or until internal temperature reaches 145° for medium rare. If desired, cook longer to achieve medium or well done meat.

Slice fennel and apples thinly and mix with arugula. Using a mandolin (preferred) or cheese grater, shred the carrot into long thin strips and add to slaw. Dress slaw with apple cider vinegar, olive oil, salt and pepper. Slice pork and serve over slaw.

Tip: For a juicy and most tender pork loin consider using a simple brine recipe before cooking.

PORTOBELLO BURGERS
WITH CHIPOTLE AIOLI

There is nothing quite as satisfying as an amazing burger and this recipe
certainly fits the bill. This juicy, full-flavor burger cooks up brilliantly
on the salt plate. Dressed with a homemade spicy aioli and fire-roasted
mushrooms this burger is truly of epic proportions. Be sure to serve the
burgers with extra aioli for dipping fries!

Burger Ingredients:

¾ lb.	ground beef
1 large	Portobello mushroom
2	lettuce leaves
½ small	red onion, thinly sliced
1 small	tomato, thinly sliced
2	brioche hamburger buns
	extra-virgin olive oil
1 tsp.	porcini powder
2	Swiss cheese slices

Chipotle Aioli Ingredients:

1 large	egg yolk
1 tsp.	Dijon mustard
2 med.	garlic cloves, minced
½ c.	extra-virgin olive oil
½ c.	grape seed or vegetable oil
1 tsp.	freshly squeezed lemon juice
¼ tsp.	kosher salt
3	chipotle peppers, seeded and minced
½ tsp.	adobo sauce (from canned chipotle peppers)
1 tsp.	Sriracha sauce

Method:

Prepare the aioli by combining egg yolk, mustard and garlic in a small bowl. While
whisking ingredients constantly, slowly begin to pour in grapeseed oil. Once the oil is fully
incorporated, add the lemon juice, minced chipotle, adobo sauce, Sriracha, and salt. Fold
until combined and set aside.

Preheat salt plate on grill as recommended on page 6. Meanwhile, mix the ground beef
with pepper and porcini powder, and divide into two separate equal sized balls. Shape
each ball of meat into a patty, brush with olive oil and set aside. Brush mushroom with
oil and set aside. When plate is fully preheated place whole mushroom in the center and
cook 5-8 minutes or until soft and tender. Flip part way through to ensure even cooking.
Remove mushroom to cutting board and cut into thin slices. Add the burger patties to the
salt plate and cook 5 to 7 minutes per side, flipping once during cooking. Add slices of
cheese on top of burgers to melt.

Toast buns directly on the grill over a medium low flame for 2-3 minutes. Garnish the
toasted buns with chipotle aioli, grilled mushroom slices, lettuce, onion, and tomato.

*Tip: To save time, aioli can be made from store bought mayonnaise and chipotle chilies.
Using this method, simply combine 2/3 cup mayo with 3 Tbsp. seeded and minced chipotle
peppers. Add ½ tsp. adobo sauce (from the canned chipotles) and mix until combined.*

PORK CHOPS
WITH MAPLE CORNBREAD STUFFING

The simplicity of cooking on a salt plate shines through in this recipe.
Succulent pork chops, seared to perfection on the soaring hot salt plate,
are accompanied by a rich, savory cornbread stuffing studded with bacon
and a good dose of maple syrup. This dish is a throwback to cool weather
comfort cooking that you'll want to make all year long.

Ingredients:

2	pork chops
1 pkg.	cornbread mix, 15 oz.
1 c.	cooked bacon, cut into ¼ inch pieces
2 Tbsp.	bacon grease (reserved from cooked bacon)
1 small	red onion, small diced
½ c.	celery, small diced
1 ½ c.	chicken stock
2 tsp.	maple syrup
1 small	egg, beaten with 1 tsp. water

Method:

Prepare cornbread mix and bake according to recipe. Cool cornbread completely and cut into
approximately ½ inch cubes. Meanwhile, add bacon grease in a medium sauté pan. Add red
onion and celery to the pan and cook gently until softened, about 7-10 minutes.

Preheat oven to 350º F. In a large mixing bowl, combine cubed cornbread, cooked bacon,
vegetables, chicken stock, and egg mixture and incorporate thoroughly. Place mixture into
a greased 8 x 8 inch baking dish. Bake stuffing at 350° F for 30 minutes or until set and
golden. While stuffing is baking, preheat salt plate on grill as recommended on page 6.
When done, remove stuffing from oven, cover with foil and set aside.

Once salt plate is preheated, place pork chops on the surface and cook for 8-10 minutes
per side or until internal temperature is at least 145° F. Serve each pork chop over warm
stuffing drizzled with 1 tsp. of maple syrup.

*Tip: Day old (or older) corn bread also works great with this recipe. To save time, prepare
corn bread the day before preparing this recipe.*

SALMON WITH MANGO SALSA AND CITRUS WILD RICE

Not only is salmon skin rich in omega 3 fatty acids, when cooked to crispy perfection on a salt plate, it's downright delectable. A perfect utilization for the salt plate, it crisps the skin and cooks the fish in just a few minutes. Paired with a sweet and spicy chutney and a hearty citrus wild rice, there's certainly nothing fishy about this elegantly easy salmon recipe.

Salmon Ingredients:

2	salmon filets, 8 ounces each

Citrus Rice Ingredients:

2 c.	water
1 c.	chicken stock
1 c.	wild rice
½ med.	orange, peel on
1 wedge	lemon

Mango Salsa Ingredients:

1 med.	mango, peeled and diced
¼ small	red onion, finely diced
1	Serrano chili pepper, seeded and finely diced
¼ c.	red bell pepper, finely diced
¼ c.	green bell pepper, finely diced
¼ c.	cilantro, chopped
½ tsp.	salt
½ tsp.	sugar
2 Tbsp.	extra-virgin olive oil
1 Tbsp.	fresh lime juice

Method:

In a medium bowl, add diced mango, red onion, bell peppers, Serrano chile, salt, sugar and olive oil. Mix well and set aside.

Preheat salt plate on grill as recommended on page 6.

Bring water, chicken stock, lemon and orange to a boil in a medium saucepan. Add wild rice and bring to a simmer. Cover and cook for 40-45 minutes until rice kernels burst open. Uncover the pan, fluff rice with a fork and cook another 5 minutes. Turn off the heat, cover the pan and set aside.

Brush salmon with olive oil and season with pepper. When the salt plate is fully preheated, place salmon onto the plate, skin side down and cook until golden and crispy, approximately 4 minutes. Flip salmon and cook another 4 minutes until internal temperature reaches 135-140° F. Serve salmon over wild rice with mango chutney.

CURRIED CHICKEN WITH JASMINE RICE

The mildly spiced curry comes together in just under an hour, making it an ideal meal choice for the entire family, any night of the week. Use boneless chicken thighs to decrease the cooking time on the salt plate and feel free to kick up the heat with additional curry paste if desired!

Chicken Curry Ingredients:

2 large	boneless skinless chicken thighs
2 Tbsp.	coconut oil
1 tsp.	fresh ginger, minced
1 tsp.	fresh garlic, minced
1 leaf	kaffir lime, minced finely
1 stalk	lemongrass, cut in half, split open

2 Tbsp.	red curry paste
5 Tbsp.	coconut cream
2 cans	coconut milk
½ tsp.	fish sauce
2 Tbsp.	brown sugar
	ground black pepper to taste
	kosher salt to taste
1 bunch	Thai basil

Rice Ingredients:

1 c.	jasmine rice, rinsed until water runs clear
1½ c.	water
½ tsp.	kosher salt

Method:

Heat the coconut oil in a medium sauté pan and add ginger, garlic, kaffir lime and lemongrass. Sauté gently for one minute or until richly fragrant. Reduce heat to low, add curry paste and continue to cook for another 2 minutes to allow flavor to mellow. Whisk in 3 Tbsp. of the coconut cream and all of the coconut milk; stir well to combine. Simmer over low heat for another 5-7 minutes. Finish by stirring in the fish sauce, brown sugar, salt and pepper. Remove from heat and set aside.

Preheat salt plate on grill as recommended on page 6. Meanwhile, prepare the rice on the stove top. Combine rice, water and salt in a medium saucepan and bring to a boil. Stir once, cover, and reduce heat to low. Simmer for 18-25 minutes.

Season chicken thighs with black pepper. Cut chicken into strips and cook on the preheated salt plate, 2-3 minutes per side until cooked through. Bring curry sauce back to a simmer and add cooked chicken, simmering 1-2 minutes.

Remove rice from heat and let stand, covered, for 5 minutes; fluff with a fork and serve with curried chicken. Garnish with remaining coconut cream and basil leaves.

DESSERTS

SEARED PEACHES WITH VANILLA RICOTTA AND BOURBON GLAZE

Your dinner crowd is going to love this gourmet version of peaches and cream! Something beautiful happens when a piece of fruit hits a blazing hot salt plate. The natural sugars of the fruit caramelize, creating a gloriously sweet and savory crust while softening the fruit's flesh ever so slightly. This recipe features an easy to make homemade ricotta and an out-of-this world caramel sauce. Add a few extra peaches to your shopping list – second helpings will be requested!

Peaches Ingredients:

2 large	peaches, halved and pitted

Ricotta Ingredients:

3 c.	whole milk
¼ tsp.	kosher salt
2 Tbsp.	distilled white vinegar or lemon juice
2	vanilla beans, halved lengthwise

Bourbon Glaze Ingredients:

¼ c.	bourbon
2 sticks	butter, softened
2 c.	light brown sugar, packed firmly
2 med.	lemons, juiced
½ c.	water

Method:

To make the ricotta, line a colander or mesh strainer with cheesecloth. Combine milk, salt, vanilla beans and vinegar or lemon juice in a microwave safe bowl. Microwave for 2-4 minutes or until mixture reaches 165° F. Remove from microwave and stir for 5 seconds. Milk should separate into curds and whey, if it does not, continue to microwave for 30 seconds until separation occurs. Skim curds from liquid and place into cheese-cloth-lined colander and let strain to desired consistency. If the ricotta becomes too dry, a small amount of milk or cream may be added in, to reconstitute.

Add bourbon to a medium saucepan and carefully boil for 30 seconds to burn off the alcohol. Add the butter, brown sugar, and water. Bring to a boil, whisking constantly until all the sugar is dissolved. Simmer for 5 minutes on medium low flame, stirring frequently. Let cool to thicken.

Preheat salt plate on grill as recommended on page 6. Placed halved peaches on preheated salt plate and sear until caramelized evenly. Serve seared peaches in small bowls with warm ricotta and a generous drizzle of bourbon glaze.

SALTED CARAMEL BANANA SPLIT

Keep a salt plate chilled in the freezer and set your imagination free when it comes to sweet and salty ice cream flavor combinations! In this recipe, a few minutes of contact with the salt plate turns caramel gelato into a salted caramel glory. Be sure to serve this communal dessert with lots of spoons – everyone will want to have a taste!

Ingredients:

1 pint	caramel gelato or ice cream
1	ripe banana
	chocolate sauce to taste
¼ c.	peanuts or almonds, toasted and chopped

Method:

Slice banana diagonally into six slices approximately ½ inch thick. Place bananas on salt plate. Place one large sized scoop of ice cream on top of bananas. Drizzle with chocolate sauce and garnish with chopped peanuts or almonds.

Tip: Don't plate this dessert too far ahead of time because the bananas will pick up too much salt from the plate. This dish also works well with brûléed bananas.

CARAMEL APPLES

A classic treat for kids and parents alike, the caramel apple is taken off of
its stick and given a salty twist in this recipe. We've formulated an easy
to make caramel sauce that tastes great drizzled on top of an apple that's
dusted with crushed peanuts.

Apples Ingredients:

2 large	Granny Smith or Fuji apples
2 Tbsp.	chopped roasted peanuts
2 small	cinnamon sticks

Caramel Sauce Ingredients:

2 Tbsp.	unsalted butter
¼ c.	cream
½ c.	brown sugar, packed firmly
1 ½ tsp.	vanilla extract

Method:

Mix brown sugar, cream, and butter in a saucepan over medium-low heat. Cook while
whisking gently 5 to 7 minutes until mixture begins to thicken. Add vanilla and cook
another minute until mixture thickens further. Remove from heat and set aside.

Slice both apples diagonally approximately ½ inch from the bottom, across the entire
width of the apple. Place the apples on the chilled salt plate, and drizzle 1 Tbsp. of sauce
on top. Garnish each apple with 1 Tbsp. of chopped peanuts and one cinnamon stick.

Thanks to all of our contributors:
Chuck Adams, Wendy Boeger, Simone Chavoor, Sarah Goodwin
Recipes by: Nick Wellhausen
Photography by: Sharon Kallenberger, Tiffany Threets
Brand design by: Natalie Torkar